Pebble® Plus

Whose Gear Is This?

by Amanda Doering Tourville

Consulting editor: Gail Saunders-Smith, PhD

CAPSTONE PRESS
a capstone imprint

Pebble Plus is published by Capstone Press,
151 Good Counsel Drive, P.O. Box 669, Mankato, Minnesota 56002.
www.capstonepub.com

Books published by Capstone Press are manufactured with paper containing at least 10 percent post-consumer waste.

Library of Congress Cataloging-in-Publication Data
Tourville, Amanda Doering, 1980-
  Whose gear is this? / by Amanda Doering Tourville.
      p. cm.—(Pebble plus. Community helper mysteries)
  Includes bibliographical references and index.
  Summary: "Simple text and full-color photographs present a mystery community helper, one clue at a time, until his or her identity is revealed"—Provided by publisher.
  ISBN 978-1-4296-6083-9 (library binding)
 1. Community life—Juvenile literature. 2. Social participation—Juvenile literature. 3. Social workers—Juvenile literature. I. Title. II. Series.
  HM771.T67 2012
  363.37—dc22   2011004618

Editorial Credits
Jeni Wittrock, editor; Matt Bruning and Bobbie Nuytten, designers; Wanda Winch, media researcher; Laura Manthe, production specialist; Sarah Schuette, photo stylist; Marcy Morin, photo scheduler

Photo Credits
All photos by Capstone Studio/Karon Dubke except:
Shutterstock: Annie Greenwood, 15, Atlaspix, 19, Melanie Kintz, cover, 1, Monkey Business Images, 7.

Capstone would like to thank the Madelia Fire Department & New Ulm Fire Department for their assistance with the photos in this book.

The editor most gratefully dedicates this book to the members of the New Ulm Fire Department, especially those on duty on February 14, 2010, who routinely risk their lives to help the community.

Note to Parents and Teachers

The Community Helper Mysteries set supports social studies standards related to communities. This book describes and illustrates firefighters. The images support early readers in understanding the text. The repetition of words and phrases helps early readers learn new words. This book also introduces early readers to subject-specific vocabulary words, which are defined in the Glossary section. Early readers may need assistance to read some words and to use the Table of Contents, Glossary, Read More, Internet Sites, and Index sections of the book.

Printed in the United States of America in North Mankato, Minnesota.
032011   006110CGF11

Table of Contents

It's a Mystery

This book is full of clues
about me. I'm a helper
in your community.
Can you guess what I do?

Here's your first clue.
I start work in a big building,
but I leave to do my job.

5

I ride in a truck. On the way to a job, I talk to my boss on my headset. My boss tells me what to do when I arrive.

Gear and Tools

I wear a suit, but not
the kind you might think.
My suit is made of layers
of heavy material.

My job takes me to

dangerous spots.

Walls and ceilings fall down.

I wear special gear to protect

my hands, head, and feet.

It can be very dark where I work.
Headlamps and spotlights help me
walk through dark places.

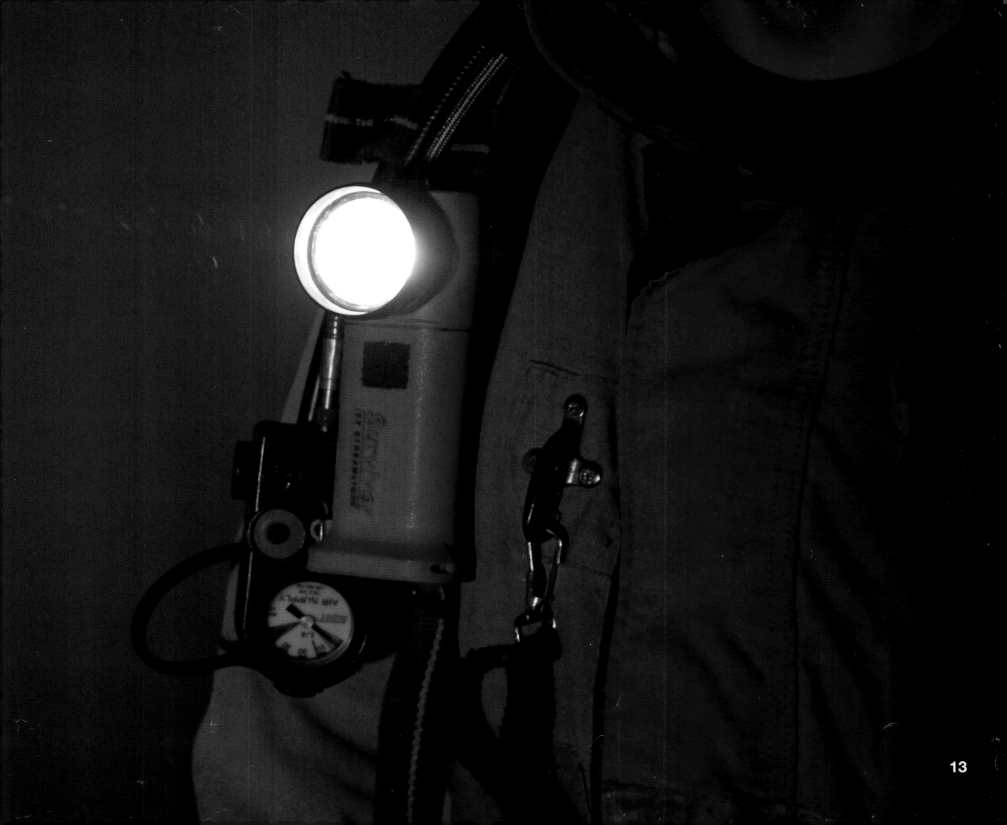

My tools help me dig, slice,

chop, and climb.

Water is an important tool I use.

How I Can Help

When there's trouble,

I rush to the scene.

If people are hurt, I help them.

I carry a first-aid kit

wherever I go.

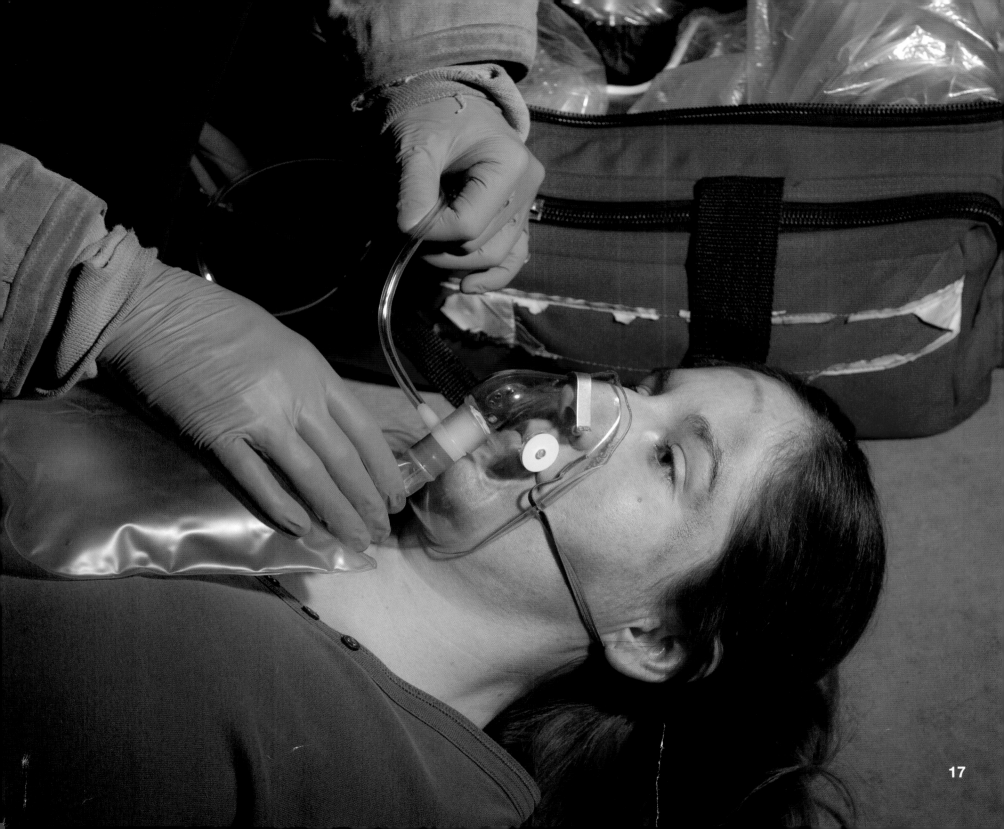

If a building starts on fire,
I will put it out. I will run
to save people and animals
trapped inside.

Have you guessed my job yet?

Mystery Solved!

I am a firefighter!

This community helper mystery
is solved.

Glossary

first-aid kit—a set of items such as bandages used to help sick or injured people

headlamp—a kind of flashlight worn on the head

headset—a pair of headphones and microphone

material—cloth or fabric; a firefighter's suit is made from a heavy material

scene—the place where an event happens

Read More

Askew, Amanda, and Andrew Crowson. *Firefighter.* People Who Help Us. Irvine, Calif.: QEB Pub., 2010.

Troupe, Thomas Kingsley. *If I Were a Firefighter.* Dream Big! Minneapolis: Picture Window Books, 2010.

Internet Sites

FactHound offers a safe, fun way to find Internet sites related to this book. All of the sites on FactHound have been researched by our staff.

Here's all you do:

Visit *www.facthound.com*

Type in this code: 9781429660839

Check out projects, games and lots more at
www.capstonekids.com

Index

Word Count: 203

Grade: 1

Early-Intervention Level: 13